W9-DHJ-710

THIS JOURNAL
BELONGS TO:

_____

NAME

_____

DATE

Rick Sarkisian, Ph.D.

The LIFEWORK PRINCIPLE Journal

Finding Meaning
in the
7 Areas of Life
that Matter Most

LifeWork
PRESS

AUTHOR'S NOTE

The contents of this Journal include adaptations
and quotes from other books I have written.

Thanks to Christopher Knuffke for his editorial contributions

©2007 LifeWork Press
All rights reserved.
ISBN: 978-0-9790825-0-4
Printed in the United States of America

Cover and graphic design by Riz Marsella
Cover Photograph © Robert Llewellyn/Corbis
Illustrations by Jim Goold

*Scripture quotations are from The Catholic Edition of the Revised Standard Version of the Bible,
©1965, ©1966 by the Division of Christian Education of the National Council of the Churches of Christ
in the United States of America. Used by permission. All rights reserved.*

www.lifeworkprinciple.com

INTRODUCTION

Why write? Why can't we just "think" about things and "remember" important events, changes and insights in our lives?

Because we don't.

In our fast-paced world, we tend to zig-zag from one responsibility to the next, frantically trying to keep pace with the many demands made on us. It's rare to have a few quiet minutes at the end of each day to just relax and reflect, let alone write.

Writing helps us refine our thoughts and gives us a reference point for where we've been and where we want to go. It's like taking pictures on a cross-country trip, creating lasting memories of the journey. For years to come, those photographs help us recall people, places and personal experiences. And writing does, too.

There is something unique about our written thoughts. The visual nature of them somehow makes them more real... more important. And these notes, if shared with future generations, will give them a uniquely personal and intimate glimpse of ourselves, our lives, our dreams, our struggles and our triumphs.

WHAT'S RIGHT ABOUT WRITING?

1. Writing disciplines the mind, helping us master and control our thoughts – one of the most difficult challenges in our human nature.

   > **Thoughts** lead to desires.
   > **Desires** leads to actions.
   > **Actions** lead to habits.
   > **Habits** shape our character.
   > **Character** determines our destiny.
   > And it all begins in the **mind**.

2. Writing, by its nature, begs us to read what we have recorded. It forces us to look at ourselves as we really are. It is the mirror of our minds. Writing humbles us by giving us visible proof of our own weakness and folly.

3. Writing is a record of graces received from God in prayer, meditation and life experiences. By writing our thoughts and spiritual experiences, we strengthen our will to remember them.

4. Writing cultivates the memory. A good memory is one that remembers what should be remembered, and forgets what should be forgotten.

5. Writing provides us with a personal moral inventory – a checklist of our victories and failures, our successes and mistakes. It helps us look back on the progress we have made (if any) in our imitation of Christ (or lack thereof).

6. Writing enhances the art of speaking. We often speak without thinking, but we can't write without thinking.

7. Writing prepares us to share our gifts with others, by keeping a visual record of our experiences, interesting episodes, successes and failures.

— based on a talk given by Rev. John Hardon

So, writing is essential in helping us commemorate, clarify and communicate our thoughts. But why use *The LifeWork Principle Journal*? Why not just use a spiral-bound notebook instead? Because *The LifeWork Principle Journal* provides a structure that helps us *collaborate* with God... to "co-labor" or "work together" with him. By choosing to build our lives in cooperation with God and his grace, rather than as individual, private dwellings, we build a secure structure that is strengthened by the graces of the Master Builder.

The LifeWork Principle Journal is all about gaining wisdom and building our lives on solid rock to withstand life's storms (see Matthew 7:24-27). We accomplish this by focusing our thoughts, words and actions on the meaningful parts of life, and writing about them within the framework of our Personal Mission Statement. Our Personal Mission Statement is, in turn, rooted in the virtues and expressed in the 7 areas of life that matter most (more on these 7 **LifeWork Areas** in a moment).

The Journal also works hand-in-hand with *The LifeWork Principle* and its focus on life-purpose. This book discusses the need to make "course corrections" to your Personal Mission Statement, readjusting and re-calibrating your life to grow in virtue and wisdom. *The LifeWork Principle Journal* will help you make those ongoing course corrections as you use it over the next 52 weeks. Ineffective, undesirable – even sinful – habits and actions will come sharply into focus allowing you to make life-changing decisions about them.

In the process of logging your thoughts and feelings about the key moments in your life, you'll gain valuable knowledge about God, yourself and your relationships with others.

With the grace of God, that knowledge can become wisdom. And holiness can grow as a result.

That is exactly what God wants of us. To be holy. To collaborate with him. To absorb more and more of his grace. To reflect the light of Christ into the darkness around us. To break free from the "gravitational pull" of the world. And it all starts when we seek to understand how our lives fit into the grand scheme of God's design.

■ Life As A Story

Have you ever thought of your life as a story - a drama played out on the stage of life – filled with interesting characters and surprising plot twists? Of course, every story or play has an **author**, and I'd like you to consider that the **primary** author of life's story is God, revealed by his Son, Jesus Christ, as our heavenly Father. He's writing the greatest story of all time – not just in the Bible, but throughout all of history – a living story that spans from creation to the end of time, and contains a distinct, irreplaceable role for each of us. It's the only story that really matters – the story that embraces all time, all events and all people. Including you and me.

But the Father isn't the **only** author of our lives. He's the **primary** author, since he holds the eternal plan for our lives and wants to be intimately involved with each of his characters. Through his grace, we are invited to "co-author" the story of our lives – to *collaborate* with the Father, the divine author, and so discover his will, his plan for our lives, as it unfolds day-by-day. So we are authors, too.

And, of course, every play or drama has **actors**, and I'd like you to consider that the **primary** actor in life's story is Jesus Christ. He is performing the role (or character) assigned to him by the author (the Father). In fact, he is part of the greatest story ever told. And it is our story too.

But Jesus isn't the **only** actor in our lives. He's the **primary** actor, since he has acted on our behalf by sacrificing himself on the cross for us. And through his grace, we are invited to "co-act" in the drama of our lives with him in self-giving love – to freely collaborate with Christ, the divine actor, in performing the role assigned to us – that is, to follow him in doing the Father's will in our daily lives. So we are actors, too.

Finally, every play has a **director**, and I'd like you to consider that the **primary** director in life's story is the Holy Spirit. He's directing the greatest story ever told – throughout all of time and space – guiding us to the truth of our existence and to eternal life.

But the Holy Spirit isn't the **only** director of our lives. He's the

primary director, since he guides us to the Father's eternal plan for our lives. Through his grace, we are invited to "co-direct" the play of our lives – to *collaborate* with the Holy Spirit, the divine director, and so accept his guidance, fulfilling the will of the Father in the story of our lives. So we are directors, too.

God gives each of us a specific and unique role in this story. But as actors in God's story or drama, does that mean we're locked into a pre-determined plot line that can't be changed? No. Because, unlike the traditional "cast of characters" in a play or drama – who are slaves to the whims and imagination of the author – we are actors who are free to collaborate in the drama – to choose, to decide, to act. Not free to determine the plot or the roles (characters), but free to be – or **not** to be – the persons God intends us to be. Free to accept or reject that God is God and we are not. Free to bring love, heroism, generosity and truthfulness to the unique roles that God has authored for us. God is able to create the story **and** leave us free in our thoughts, words and actions – free to interpret the text of the author (the Father); free to follow Jesus and collaborate with him; and free to interpret the promptings of the director (the Holy Spirit).

■ WE LONG TO BELONG

As free characters, we can pursue happiness and joy and satisfaction however we choose. But to be truly fulfilled characters in God's story, we must learn what it means to "belong," choosing to give ourselves either to God or the world. There are lots of ways to belong. Many of the characters in God's story choose to belong to power, position or pride – all types of slavery. Yet others discover a deep sense of belonging built upon a lifelong partnership with Christ and his church... a belonging that becomes evident in our lives through strong relationships and balance in the areas of life that matter most.

So what about all the other people and their roles (characters) in God's grand story? They are also part of the story of our lives. In God's plan, we are not isolated individuals; we are all called to belong to God's family. We are closely interconnected to the other actors – the "cast of characters" in our lives.

They, like us, are called to collaborate with God – with the Holy Spirit directing them in fulfilling the Father's will. Every person in our lives has a different role (character) to play, yet they help us to define and fulfill our own roles. These characters – as well as the events and circumstances we encounter in the story – give relevance to our roles.

If you see yourself as the only author, actor and director in your story, life becomes a "do-it-yourself" project with no instructions, no sense of a master plan. It's like building your house without a blueprint. The results may leave you unfulfilled and very disappointed. The house may collapse.

But if you see yourself as part of a grand story in which you are free to collaborate with the other characters and, indeed, with the author himself, then life takes on true purpose and direction. You'll be building your house on rock based on God's divine blueprint (the Bible). As a result, you'll be well on your way to ultimate fulfillment and lasting satisfaction.

If you choose to separate yourself from the unique, unrepeatable plan God has designed for your life, then you may never experience the joy and purpose life has to offer. It's like choosing to watch a black-and-white television with fuzzy reception and a tiny speaker, instead of a large-screen television with vivid color and surround sound!

But the Father hasn't finished his story yet, and he hasn't chiseled the plot in stone. And if we are "good" characters, accepting the Holy Spirit's guidance, we will follow Christ day-by-day in making wise and beneficial decisions, fulfilling the Father's will in our lives.

God's story is already filled with his grace – and with his truth, beauty and goodness – and the characters serve to reveal Christ's presence – his love and mercy. When, by his grace, we actively collaborate with God, the Holy Spirit will direct us in the daily decisions we make.

But what if we turn away from God, and make selfish, sinful choices? Then we can turn back to God and ask for his mercy and forgiveness. Through his Son, Jesus Christ, we can receive pardon and peace, and start afresh.

To restore and re-establish our lives in Christ, God "edits the story." He makes changes – for our own good – when we contradict God's nature and his eternal plan for us. And since his story involves a whole "cast of characters," our choices affect them as well – for better or for worse. To be a follower of Christ means to begin again, over and over... fortunately for us!

■ Who Do You Want To Be?

What kind of characters will we be in God's story? That's for us to decide, based on selfishness or on the self-giving love of Jesus. We determine how we will interact with other characters, each one living out the "subplot" in which God has placed them.

Each subplot is equally worthy and important before God – whether it involves an impoverished family, a wealthy entrepreneur, a convicted criminal, a homeless veteran, a brave rescue worker, an abandoned orphan or a doting grandparent. Likewise, each character is equally worthy and important. Why? Because we are all equal before God – and he loves each one of us infinitely. And because Christ died for each one of us.

If we don't believe that, then our worldview narrows, elevating some characters above others. The successful executive becomes far more impressive than the relapsed drug addict. The professional athlete has greater value than a migrant farm worker. But when we see these characters from an eternal perspective, things look different.

You get the point! It all comes down to changing our perceptions and actions, based on divine grace and on our understanding of the author's story and our roles in Christ. It's exciting! Especially since the author doesn't show us the whole story at any one time – instead he reveals it to us gradually in the Holy Spirit and through his Word: page-by-page, chapter-by-chapter, as we journey through life – making daily, grace-filled decisions in the 7 areas of life that matter most.

■ OUR PERMANENT PAST

Perhaps the most daunting thing about seeing our lives as stories rather than projects is that we can no longer ignore our past. It's always right there in "black and white." Unerasable. Unchangeable. Painful events remain forever a part of the story of our lives.

But with God's help, we don't need to erase or change the past. Instead, Christ can *transform* the meaning of our past and let events remain as they were. All we need to do is ask God for his mercy and forgiveness for our past failings and sins; resolve to change by the help of his grace; and ask him to bring good out of evil. Success from failure. Healing from pain. "With God, all things are possible" (see Matthew 19:26).

Then we can give our freedom to our heavenly Father. By giving him our freedom, we let him inhabit our choices – so that we act with love, honesty, courage and caring. In essence, we give our free will back to God as a gift! When we do that, we become fully involved in a story with infinite, eternal fullness – a grace-filled drama that can touch the whole "cast of characters" around us.

Giving our free will back to God as a gift – that's a radical concept that can lead us to a radically changed life!

■ TIME AND ETERNITY

We are rapidly moving through time and space toward an eventual encounter with God himself. As we journey through God's story and toward eternity, *The LifeWork Principle Journal* can be our spiritual notebook. It is a tool for recording our insights and reflections about God's grace at work in our lives, but it is also much more than that. It is a double-door opened wide to allow us to step into God's story, to collaborate with him, and to make commitments for real, lasting change. We'll have the opportunity in these pages to set life-changing goals in prayerful partnership with Christ and make written commitments to achieve them.

The LifeWork Principle Journal allows us to view time within an eternal perspective. In other words, what we do (or don't do) affects our role in God's story and thus has eternal consequences. As a result, the Journal will not only help us stay on track on our earthly journey to eternal life, but also help us examine how wisely we have used the gift of time each week.

■ PERSONAL MISSION STATEMENT

Your Personal Mission Statement is a clear, brief statement of what you are all about... who you can and should be according to God's design. It becomes a roadmap for your journey to heaven. Like a map, your Personal Mission Statement gives you a reference point for staying on course and lets you know if corrections should be made.

Defining your mission and purpose in life involves learning how to serve God in thoughts, words and actions, wherever you find yourself. Remember, God has a unique, specific and highly personal purpose for your life — a particular way to follow Jesus — and he reveals that purpose over the course of your lifetime.

Seeking God's call can help you discover your vocation (to be who God wants you to be) and your mission (to do what God wants you to do) in life.

Your **vocation** is made up of two parts: the *General Call* to live a holy life, and the *Specific Call* to a unique life-commitment such as marriage, the single life or the clergy. Likewise, your **mission** is composed of two parts: the *General Witness* to others of Christ, and your *LifeWork Choices* – the specific use of God-given abilities to give glory to him in all aspects of your life.

Your Personal Mission Statement allows you to revisit on a weekly basis the direction you have prayerfully discovered, making adjustments by God's grace as you gain knowledge and wisdom of his will.

Determine how you can serve God in the home, church and world. Make this a starting point for developing your Personal Mission Statement.

EXAMPLE 1:

- In the home, I will live by the virtues of humility and kindness and help others to grow closer to Christ.
- In the church, I will serve God by a devout life and pray regularly for the needs of others.
- In the world, I will help the poor with my time and resources, sharing my God-given talents.

EXAMPLE 2:

- I will place God at the center of my life.
- I will be a witness of Christ's love through the virtues of humility and kindness.
- I will pray daily for the needs of others and serve the poor.
- I will keep an eternal perspective in all matters of life.

EXAMPLE 3:

- I will seek God's will in my thoughts, words and actions.
- I will be an example of hope, trust and Christian commitment.
- I will treat everyone with Christ-like love and acceptance.

Your Personal Mission Statement is not – and should not be – chiseled in stone. Because of changing circumstances, your Personal Mission Statement requires flexibility. The solid, unchanging principles you've established sometimes need to be applied differently, depending on what's going on in your life. So don't be afraid to make changes to it in order to "realign" your life as God continuously unfolds his plan for you. Review your Personal Mission Statement regularly and make adjustments as needed!

IN MY HOME...

IN THE CHURCH...

IN THE WORLD...

❧ The 7 LifeWork Areas ❧

In *The LifeWork Principle*, I introduced the idea that there are 7 areas of life that matter most, each having value based on the choices we make and our particular lifestyle. I call them the **7 LifeWork Areas.** Each day, as we live out our vocation and mission in life, we allocate time to these areas, either using it well or using it poorly.

The 7 LifeWork Areas are:

1. **FAITH:** Believing that God is active in every aspect of the story of your life.

2. **RELATIONSHIPS:** Appreciating your own story as well as creatively collaborating with God and the "cast of characters" you encounter in your story.

3. **WORK:** Understanding how the Father has *equipped* you for your story and *sent* you out in a specific role to accomplish your work. And then doing it.

4. **KNOWLEDGE:** Learning how you and your role fit into the grand story of life.

5. **SOCIETY:** Helping others, the "cast of characters," as your story unfolds.

6. **FITNESS:** Keeping yourself strong and healthy in body, mind and spirit.

7. **LEISURE:** Regularly slowing down the pace of your story to give yourself rest and relaxation.

Your *LifeWork* is not just about your job or career. It includes all you do in the **7 LifeWork Areas** through the balanced allocation of time, skills, personal qualities and interests. This helps define who you are as a son or daughter of Christ. In this Journal, you will be asked to consider these 7 areas weekly.

■ COMMITMENT

The process of using *The LifeWork Principle Journal* is more important than the specific results. Why? Because outcomes and "success" are God's business, not ours. Our responsibility is to make our best efforts with the help of God's grace. In your journal, you'll be asked to make commitments each week in the 7 **LifeWork Areas**. This will help you adjust your behaviors and activities and point you in the direction of your desired outcomes. Don't worry if you don't achieve those outcomes as quickly as you'd like, or at all. Leave the outcomes to God. Just do your part and trust God to do his... in his way, and in his timing.

To get the most out of *The LifeWork Principle Journal*, go beyond just making journal entries. Consider Bible readings as guidelines for each week – nourishment for your daily prayer life. Take the time to contemplate Christ, to meditate on God's Word in Scripture, and pray each day. Also, read good spiritual books and spend time with other believers, especially in community worship.

■ THE 7 LIFEWORK ROLES

In the story of your life, why accept and live out various roles, responsibilities and personal qualities? To live out our mission and purpose in life more closely, because WHO we are – the quality of our character – greatly impacts WHAT we can do in all 7 **LifeWork Areas**. Select a specific role and personal quality each week that will be a particular focus for you, so that you can practice it and turn it into a habit. It helps to think of a person you know or a historical figure that embodies this role and quality (a role model). As a reminder of your commitment to change, place the role, a role model and personal quality in the "Weekly Focus" box. You can change the focus each week, or repeat it for as many weeks as you believe necessary.

In addition to the general role of following Christ and the personal qualities of faith, hope and charity (love), here are the 7 **LifeWork Roles** and their related personal qualities to consider:

VISIONARY
☐ Creativity
☐ Simplicity
☐ Influence
☐ Purposefulness

OPTIMIST
☐ Humor
☐ Cheerfulness
☐ Joyfulness
☐ Hope

COMMUNICATOR
☐ Passion
☐ Enthusiasm
☐ Prayerfulness
☐ Honesty

COACH
☐ Self-discipline
☐ Integrity
☐ Perseverance
☐ Leadership

FRIEND
☐ Trust
☐ Tolerance
☐ Unselfishness
☐ Empathy

PEACEMAKER
☐ Forgiveness
☐ Respect
☐ Patience
☐ Calmness

SERVANT
☐ Sacrifice
☐ Humility
☐ Kindness
☐ Compassion

THE LIFEWORK DISCOVERY PROCESS

As each week comes to an end, take time to look back on the prior week ("review") <u>and</u> look ahead to the coming week ("preview"). Not only can this process help you determine how your life measures up to your Personal Mission Statement, it can take you to exciting new levels of discovery and discernment! Here's how it works:

REVIEW THE PRIOR WEEK:

1. PRAY FOR THE GUIDANCE OF THE HOLY SPIRIT.

   Ask the Holy Spirit to fill your life with truth, knowledge, insight and wisdom as you go over the events, experiences and emotions of the past week.

   Come Holy Spirit. Fill my heart, mind and soul with wisdom, truth and the fire of your love so that I can follow Jesus more closely and more fully embrace God's presence in my life. Amen.

2. TAKE A MORAL INVENTORY OF YOUR THOUGHTS, WORDS AND ACTIONS (GOOD AND BAD) OF THE PAST WEEK.

   Examine your conscience for what you have done and what you have failed to do in thoughts, words and actions.

   Were your thoughts pure, hopeful and loving or have you given in to impurity, worry, envy and anxiety?

   Were your words kind, constructive and positive or have they been destructive, judgmental, negative and critical?

   Were your actions generous, humble and caring or selfish, angry or prideful?

3. OFFER PRAISE AND THANKSGIVING FOR THE GRACES YOU HAVE RECEIVED.

Express your gratitude for God's fatherly presence in your life and the blessings freely given to you.

Heavenly Father, I offer you my praise and thanksgiving for all the blessings in my life, especially in this past week. With deep humility, I thank you for the opportunity to be your child and servant through your Son, Jesus. Amen.

4. OFFER SORROW FOR YOUR FAILINGS AND SINS, AND ASK FOR GOD'S MERCY AND FORGIVENESS.

Acknowledge your failings and shortcomings, expressing sorrow and repentance for them, and seeking God's forgiveness.

My God, I am sorry for my sins with all my heart. For choosing to do wrong and failing to do good, I have sinned against you, whom I should love above all things. I firmly intend to sin no more and to avoid whatever leads me to sin. I ask for your mercy and forgiveness through your Son, Jesus. Amen.

5. RESOLVE, WITH THE HELP OF GOD'S GRACE, TO AVOID SIN AND STRIVE FOR MORAL EXCELLENCE IN THE **7 LIFEWORK AREAS.**

Make firm commitments about the person you'll be in the week to come; about what you will do and not do with the help of God's grace.

Lord, I recommit myself to you this week in all my prayers, works, ups and downs. Help me be the person you want me to be and do the things you want me to do. Amen.

1. CHECK YOUR PERSONAL MISSION STATEMENT
    FOR NEEDED ADJUSTMENTS.

    Are course corrections necessary? Do you need to recalibrate
    the scope and direction of your mission statement? Based
    on solid, unchanging principles, it may be necessary that the
    focus of your life-purpose and mission be expressed in fresh,
    new ways within the context of your mission statement.

2. THINK THROUGH THE COMING WEEK IN LIGHT OF
    THE **7 LIFEWORK AREAS**.

    What are the events and circumstances that will affect you
    in the areas of faith, relationships, work, knowledge, society,
    fitness and leisure?

    How can you create a deeper level of satisfaction by wisely
    allocating time to these 7 areas? How "balanced" do you
    see yourself in the week to come?

3. SET GOALS AND MAKE COMMITMENTS IN
    THE **7 LIFEWORK AREAS**.

    Establish measurable and attainable goals, then make a
    journal resolution to achieve your goals with God's help in
    the 7 areas of life that matter most.

    My Lord and my God, help me discover, develop and use
    the gifts and talents you have freely offered and make the
    best use of my abilities. May I always use your gifts in
    humility, obedience, and for your honor and glory. Help me
    to establish firm resolutions and commitments about life
    that allow me to grow closer to Jesus and stay on the path
    to eternal life. Amen.

4. ASK FOR THE GRACE TO LIVE THESE
   COMMITMENTS.

   You can't do it alone! With God's grace, you can remain on
   the straight path that keeps you pointed towards eternal life.
   It is with God's grace that you can accomplish small things
   and great things.

   *Jesus, the source of all grace, I ask that you increase your
   divine presence within me. Help me to open my heart, mind
   and soul more fully to your presence and help me grow in
   the virtues of faith, hope and love. Amen.*

5. RESOLVE TO FOLLOW CHRIST AND LIVE OUT
   A PARTICULAR ROLE AND PERSONAL QUALITY
   EACH WEEK.

   Prayerfully choose a particular role and personal quality
   from the list shown on page 14, noting them in your journal
   for the week. Ask God's help in practicing your selection
   daily with others.

   *Lord, help me to live the role of_____and personal quality
   of_____in the week to come. Give me the grace to follow
   Jesus more closely. I will try to do my best in knowing,
   loving and serving you each day with the help of your grace.
   Amen.*

Let's Get Started !

It's time to start writing! Get ready to list your weekly commitments for the **7 LifeWork Areas** within the context of your Personal Mission Statement, choose a role, a role model and personal quality for the week and remain focused on Christ within your home, the church and the world. There's also a special place each week where you can list any key insights gained through The LifeWork Discovery Process. These insights can be gathered through personal prayer, spiritual reading, observations and internal inspirations of the Holy Spirit.

Your journal entries can relate to how effectively you live up to the standards of your Personal Mission Statement, and the insights you derive from God's grace and your actions.

May God richly bless you as you collaborate with him on the story of your life!

Rick Sarkisian

·

Commitments

FAITH

RELATIONSHIPS

WORK

KNOWLEDGE

SOCIETY

FITNESS

LEISURE

*T*HERE'S A
CERTAIN BEAUTY —
A REAL FREEDOM —
IN MAINTAINING
AN ETERNAL
PERSPECTIVE.

WEEK 2

Commitments

FAITH

RELATIONSHIPS

WORK

KNOWLEDGE

SOCIETY

FITNESS

LEISURE

OUR LIFEWORK
SPANS THE COURSE
OF OUR LIFETIME,
AND CAN BE LIVED
OUT IN EVERY ASPECT
OF OUR LIVES.

KEY INSIGHTS

WEEK *3*

Commitments

FAITH

RELATIONSHIPS

WORK

KNOWLEDGE

SOCIETY

FITNESS

LEISURE

*G*OD WANTS JUST
ONE THING FROM
EACH OF US:
EVERYTHING...
TO SURRENDER OUR
LIVES TO HIM.

KEY INSIGHTS

Commitments

FAITH

RELATIONSHIPS

WORK

KNOWLEDGE

SOCIETY

FITNESS

LEISURE

*Y*OUR WORK
BECOMES A DAILY
"THANK YOU" TO THE
ONE WHO EQUIPPED YOU
WITH THE TALENTS,
GIFTS AND ABILITIES
THAT ENABLE YOU
TO WORK IN THE
FIRST PLACE!

_____

_____

_____

_____

_____

_____

_____

_____

_____

_____

KEY INSIGHTS

_____

_____

_____

_____

WEEK 5

Commitments

FAITH

RELATIONSHIPS

WORK

KNOWLEDGE

SOCIETY

FITNESS

LEISURE

THE WORLD AROUND YOU WILL SEEM BROADER AND LARGER THAN YOU NOTICED BEFORE BECAUSE YOU WILL HAVE ESTABLISHED A CREATIVE PARTNERSHIP WITH GOD. YOUR CAPACITY TO EMBRACE LIFE INCREASES.

WEEK *6*

Commitments

FAITH

RELATIONSHIPS

WORK

KNOWLEDGE

SOCIETY

FITNESS

LEISURE

*M*AKE LEARNING
A LIFETIME PROCESS.
SEEK NEW INFORMATION
AND KNOWLEDGE
EVERYDAY. YOUR
BRAIN CAN HANDLE IT!

Week 7

Commitments

FAITH

RELATIONSHIPS

WORK

KNOWLEDGE

SOCIETY

FITNESS

LEISURE

*G*o INTO THE
VINEYARD OF LIFE
AND ENJOY THE
SATISFACTION OF
HELPING OTHERS
LESS FORTUNATE
THAN YOU.

LIFEWORK ROLE

ROLE MODEL

PERSONAL QUALITY

WEEK *8*

Commitments

FAITH

RELATIONSHIPS

WORK

KNOWLEDGE

SOCIETY

FITNESS

LEISURE

WHAT WE KNOW
DETERMINES
HOW WE THINK,
AND HOW WE THINK
AFFECTS HOW
WE FEEL. THOUGHTS
TRAVEL QUICKLY
FROM THE HEAD
TO THE HEART.

LifeWork Role

Role Model

Personal Quality

WEEK *9*

Commitments

FAITH

RELATIONSHIPS

WORK

KNOWLEDGE

SOCIETY

FITNESS

LEISURE

THE MORE WE
KNOW ABOUT THE
WORLD, THE MORE
WE KNOW ABOUT THE
GOD WHO CREATED IT.
LIFE IS ABOUT
KNOWING, LOVING AND
SERVING THE GOD
WHO MADE US.

Week 10

Commitments

FAITH

RELATIONSHIPS

WORK

KNOWLEDGE

SOCIETY

FITNESS

LEISURE

THE MORE WE COME
TO KNOW GOD, THE
MORE WE WILL TRUST
HIM IN ALL THINGS.

LIFEWORK ROLE

ROLE MODEL

PERSONAL QUALITY

WEEK *11*

Commitments

FAITH

RELATIONSHIPS

WORK

KNOWLEDGE

SOCIETY

FITNESS

LEISURE

WE ARE ON AN
EARTHLY JOURNEY
TO THE FATHER. THE
CHOICES WE MAKE, THE
STEPS WE TAKE, WILL
EITHER LEAD US TO HIM
OR AWAY FROM HIM.

LifeWork Role

Role Model

Personal Quality

WEEK *12*

Commitments

FAITH

RELATIONSHIPS

WORK

KNOWLEDGE

SOCIETY

FITNESS

LEISURE

*A*LLOW GOD TO
CHALLENGE OUR
COMFORTABLE LIVES.
ASK HIM WHAT WE
CAN DO TO FILL THE
NEEDS OF OTHERS.

KEY INSIGHTS

WEEK *13*

Commitments

FAITH

RELATIONSHIPS

WORK

KNOWLEDGE

SOCIETY

FITNESS

LEISURE

*I*T ALL COMES DOWN
TO THIS QUESTION:
WILL YOU LIVE A
SELF-CENTERED LIFE OR
A LIFE THAT EXTENDS
ITS BRANCHES, SHADE
AND FRUITFULNESS TO
THOSE IN THE WORLD
AROUND YOU?

LifeWork Role

Role Model

Personal Quality

Commitments

FAITH

RELATIONSHIPS

WORK

KNOWLEDGE

SOCIETY

FITNESS

LEISURE

You will
experience great
satisfaction in living
an active faith,
allowing Christ to
use you as a vessel,
pouring out his love,
mercy and goodness
over the world.

LIFEWORK ROLE

ROLE MODEL

PERSONAL QUALITY

WEEK *15*

Commitments

_____

_____

_____

_____

_____

_____

_____

_____

FAITH

RELATIONSHIPS

WORK

KNOWLEDGE

SOCIETY

FITNESS

LEISURE

To keep it all in perspective, view heaven as our true home and earth as our land in exile. We live a temporary existence here, but all that we do on earth has eternal consequences.

KEY INSIGHTS

Commitments

FAITH

RELATIONSHIPS

WORK

KNOWLEDGE

SOCIETY

FITNESS

LEISURE

The less you have, the less you have to worry about. Less really is more!

Commitments

FAITH

RELATIONSHIPS

WORK

KNOWLEDGE

SOCIETY

FITNESS

LEISURE

*S*ILENCE IS THE
CLASSROOM OF PRAYER.

LIFEWORK ROLE

ROLE MODEL

PERSONAL QUALITY

Week 18

Commitments

FAITH

RELATIONSHIPS

WORK

KNOWLEDGE

SOCIETY

FITNESS

LEISURE

*S*TAYING ON COURSE
DEPENDS LARGELY
ON STAYING FIT AND
BALANCED IN THE 7
LifeWork Areas.

WEEK *19*

Commitments

FAITH

RELATIONSHIPS

WORK

KNOWLEDGE

SOCIETY

FITNESS

LEISURE

LIKE EVERYTHING
ELSE AROUND US, THE
DIMENSIONS OF BODY,
MIND AND SPIRIT ARE
UNIQUE GIFTS FROM GOD
WHO CREATED US...
TO PROVIDE THE MEANS
FOR BEING WHO GOD
WANTS US TO BE AND
DOING WHAT GOD
WANTS US TO DO.

KEY INSIGHTS

WEEK *20*

Commitments

FAITH

RELATIONSHIPS

WORK

KNOWLEDGE

SOCIETY

FITNESS

LEISURE

*A*SK THE HOLY SPIRIT
FOR THE GRACE
TO KNOW WHAT
YOU SHOULD DO TO
HELP OTHERS.

WEEK *21*

Commitments

FAITH

RELATIONSHIPS

WORK

KNOWLEDGE

SOCIETY

FITNESS

LEISURE

To keep your emotional thermostat in balance, think of the word "HALT" as an acronym, which can remind you to adjust your thermostat when you are Hungry, Angry, Lonely or Tired.

WEEK 22

Commitments

FAITH

RELATIONSHIPS

WORK

KNOWLEDGE

SOCIETY

FITNESS

LEISURE

OUR SPIRITUAL
LIFE REQUIRES
REGULAR
NOURISHMENT.

WEEK *23*

Commitments

FAITH

RELATIONSHIPS

WORK

KNOWLEDGE

SOCIETY

FITNESS

LEISURE

*P*RACTICING PATIENCE
AND HUMILITY IS
LIKE PRACTICING
PHYSICAL EXERCISE
– IT'S CHALLENGING
BUT EFFECTIVE. THE
MORE CHALLENGING
THE EXERCISE, THE
STRONGER YOU BECOME.

WEEKLY FOCUS

LIFEWORK ROLE

ROLE MODEL

PERSONAL QUALITY

WEEK 24

Commitments

FAITH

RELATIONSHIPS

WORK

KNOWLEDGE

SOCIETY

FITNESS

LEISURE

*T*HERE IS A DIRECT
AND PROPORTIONATE
RELATIONSHIP BETWEEN
THE QUALITY OF OUR
LEISURE TIME AND ALL
THE OTHER LifeWork
AREAS. AS WE IMPROVE,
INCREASE AND EXPAND
THE LEISURE IN OUR
LIFE, WE FIND THAT THE
WORLD AROUND US GETS
BIGGER AND BRIGHTER.

KEY INSIGHTS

WEEK 25

Commitments

FAITH

RELATIONSHIPS

WORK

KNOWLEDGE

SOCIETY

FITNESS

LEISURE

*P*ARTICIPATE IN
THE RELENTLESS
PURSUIT OF... HUMOR!
THE MORE WE ENGAGE
IN GOOD HUMOR,
THE MORE LIKELY WE
ARE TO DEVELOP A
POSITIVE DISPOSITION
OF CHEERFULNESS —
BEING MORE UPBEAT,
OPTIMISTIC AND PRONE
TO SMILING.

WEEK *26*

Commitments

FAITH

RELATIONSHIPS

WORK

KNOWLEDGE

SOCIETY

FITNESS

LEISURE

*C*USTODY OF
THE HEART BEGINS
WITH CUSTODY OF
THE EYES.

LIFEWORK ROLE

ROLE MODEL

PERSONAL QUALITY

Commitments

FAITH

RELATIONSHIPS

WORK

KNOWLEDGE

SOCIETY

FITNESS

LEISURE

*O*UR DECISIONS
ABOUT LIFE PASS
THROUGH THE FILTER
OF OUR BELIEFS
AND MORALS. AND
WHAT WE <u>DO</u> REVEALS
THE "VIRTUES"
IN OUR LIFE.

WEEK *28*

Commitments

FAITH

RELATIONSHIPS

WORK

KNOWLEDGE

SOCIETY

FITNESS

LEISURE

*P*ATIENCE IS THE
VIRTUE THAT ALLOWS
US TO QUIETLY
PERSEVERE IN THE
FACE OF TROUBLES
AND PROVOCATION.
THE FRUITS OF
PRACTICING THE VIRTUE
OF PATIENCE INCLUDE:
LESS VOLATILITY IN
OUR RELATIONSHIPS,
LESS STRESS IN OUR LIFE,
AND A GREATER SENSE
OF ENDURING
SELF-CONTROL.

LIFEWORK ROLE

ROLE MODEL

PERSONAL QUALITY

Week 29

Commitments

FAITH

RELATIONSHIPS

WORK

KNOWLEDGE

SOCIETY

FITNESS

LEISURE

To BECOME MORE
HUMBLE, CAN WE
EMPTY OUR EGOS AND
GIVE CREDIT TO GOD
FOR ALL THAT HAPPENS
IN OUR LIFE?

LIFEWORK ROLE

ROLE MODEL

PERSONAL QUALITY

KEY INSIGHTS

WEEK *30*

Commitments

FAITH

RELATIONSHIPS

WORK

KNOWLEDGE

SOCIETY

FITNESS

LEISURE

It's within a simple, ordinary life that we can discover daily opportunities for holiness. And become extraordinary in ordinary things.

Week 31

Commitments

FAITH

RELATIONSHIPS

WORK

KNOWLEDGE

SOCIETY

FITNESS

LEISURE

*O*BEDIENCE
REQUIRES THE HEART
OF A CHILD AND THE
MIND OF A SERVANT...
TO SERVE GOD AS AN
EXPRESSION OF OUR
FREE WILL.

LifeWork Role

Role Model

Personal Quality

WEEK *32*

Commitments

FAITH

RELATIONSHIPS

WORK

KNOWLEDGE

SOCIETY

FITNESS

LEISURE

*C*OURSE CORRECTIONS — MADE THROUGH A STRONG SPIRITUAL LIFE, FORTIFIED BY DAILY PRAYER — ARE NECESSARY FOR OUR SPIRITUAL JOURNEY.

LifeWork Role

Role Model

Personal Quality

Week *33*

Commitments

Faith

Relationships

Work

Knowledge

Society

Fitness

Leisure

*O*UR CHARACTER
IS DEFINED
BY THE CHOICES
WE MAKE.

LIFEWORK ROLE

ROLE MODEL

PERSONAL QUALITY

KEY INSIGHTS

Week *34*

Commitments

FAITH

RELATIONSHIPS

WORK

KNOWLEDGE

SOCIETY

FITNESS

LEISURE

*G*OD CALLS US
TO BE BRAVE,
EVEN FEARLESS;
UNYIELDING TO THE
PRESSURE OF THE
SECULAR WORLD THAT
SURROUNDS US.

LIFEWORK ROLE

ROLE MODEL

PERSONAL QUALITY

KEY INSIGHTS

WEEK 35

Commitments

FAITH

RELATIONSHIPS

WORK

KNOWLEDGE

SOCIETY

FITNESS

LEISURE

A DEEP, PROFOUND
FAITH LEADS US TO
LOVE GOD FOR WHO HE
IS, RATHER THAN WHAT
HE CAN DO FOR US.

KEY INSIGHTS

WEEK *36*

Commitments

FAITH

RELATIONSHIPS

WORK

KNOWLEDGE

SOCIETY

FITNESS

LEISURE

*W*E HAVE THE
AMAZING OPPORTUNITY
TO DAILY DEMONSTRATE
OUR COMMITMENT TO
WORK, FAMILY AND
FAITH. REMAINING
STEADFAST IN OUR
FOCUS ON GOD.
WORKING AS AN
EXPRESSION OF LOVE
FOR OUR FAMILY.

LifeWork Role

Role Model

Personal Quality

WEEK *37*

Commitments

FAITH

RELATIONSHIPS

WORK

KNOWLEDGE

SOCIETY

FITNESS

LEISURE

*O*UR GOAL IS TO
"LAND" SAFELY
IN GOD'S ETERNAL
KINGDOM, RELYING ON
HIS "GUIDANCE SYSTEM"
OF FAITH, HOPE
AND LOVE.

WEEK *38*

Commitments

FAITH

RELATIONSHIPS

WORK

KNOWLEDGE

SOCIETY

FITNESS

LEISURE

ARE WE WILLING TO SUBMIT TO GOD'S WILL IN SUCH A WAY THAT WE CONSTANTLY SEEK HIS GUIDANCE? ARE WE WILLING TO <u>COLLABORATE</u> — TO WORK WITH HIM — SO THAT HIS PLAN FOR OUR LIVES CAN BE IMPLEMENTED?

Commitments

FAITH

RELATIONSHIPS

WORK

KNOWLEDGE

SOCIETY

FITNESS

LEISURE

$\mathcal{T}$HERE IS
SOMETHING UNIQUE
ABOUT OUR WRITTEN
THOUGHTS. THE
VISUAL NATURE OF
THEM SOMEHOW
MAKES THEM MORE
REAL... MORE
IMPORTANT.

LifeWork Role

Role Model

Personal Quality

WEEK 40

Commitments

FAITH

RELATIONSHIPS

WORK

KNOWLEDGE

SOCIETY

FITNESS

LEISURE

*W*E ARE ACCOUNTABLE TO GOD FOR OUR ACTIONS.

WEEK *41*

Commitments

FAITH

RELATIONSHIPS

WORK

KNOWLEDGE

SOCIETY

FITNESS

LEISURE

*W*E RELY WITH
CONFIDENCE ON GOD,
WHO IS <u>ALWAYS</u>
WITH US IN
TROUBLED TIMES.

KEY INSIGHTS

WEEK *42*

Commitments

FAITH

RELATIONSHIPS

WORK

KNOWLEDGE

SOCIETY

FITNESS

LEISURE

WITH GOD'S GRACE,
WE WILL PREVAIL IN THE
BATTLE FOR PURITY.

WEEKLY FOCUS

LifeWork Role

Role Model

Personal Quality

WEEK 43

Commitments

_____

_____

_____

_____

_____

_____

_____

_____

FAITH

RELATIONSHIPS

WORK

KNOWLEDGE

SOCIETY

FITNESS

LEISURE

_____

_____

_____

_____

_____

*N*O RELATIONSHIP
CAN GROW WITHOUT
COMMUNICATION,
AND PRAYER OPENS
THE LINES OF
COMMUNICATION
BETWEEN YOU AND
YOUR CREATOR.
THERE IS NO GREATER
RELATIONSHIP YOU
CAN ENTER THAN
THIS ONE!

_____

_____

_____

_____

_____

_____

_____

_____

_____

_____

_____

KEY INSIGHTS

_____

_____

_____

_____

_____

WEEK 44

Commitments

_____

_____

_____

_____

_____

_____

_____

_____

_____ FAITH

_____ RELATIONSHIPS

_____ WORK

_____ KNOWLEDGE

_____ SOCIETY

_____ FITNESS

_____ LEISURE

_____

_____

_____

WE DON'T KNOW
WHAT THE FUTURE
HOLDS, BUT WE
KNOW WHO HOLDS
THE FUTURE!

KEY INSIGHTS

WEEK 45

Commitments

FAITH

RELATIONSHIPS

WORK

KNOWLEDGE

SOCIETY

FITNESS

LEISURE

*I*F YOU DON'T
DEFINE YOUR
MISSION IN LIFE,
THE WORLD WILL.

LifeWork Role

Role Model

Personal Quality

KEY INSIGHTS

WEEK *46*

Commitments

FAITH

RELATIONSHIPS

WORK

KNOWLEDGE

SOCIETY

FITNESS

LEISURE

*L*EARN TO LAUGH
HEARTILY, SMILE
FREQUENTLY AND SHARE
YOUR CHEERFUL NATURE
GENEROUSLY WITH
THOSE AROUND YOU.

KEY INSIGHTS

Commitments

FAITH

RELATIONSHIPS

WORK

KNOWLEDGE

SOCIETY

FITNESS

LEISURE

*O*UR SPECIFIC
MISSION IS TO USE
OUR SKILLS, VIRTUES
AND SPIRITUAL
GIFTS TO HONOR
GOD IN EVERYTHING
WE DO. THIS IS OUR
"LIFEWORK."

WEEK 48

Commitments

FAITH

RELATIONSHIPS

WORK

KNOWLEDGE

SOCIETY

FITNESS

LEISURE

$\mathscr{D}$ISCOVERING YOUR
PERSONAL VOCATION
AND MISSION ISN'T
A SINGLE, ONCE-AND-
FOR-ALL EVENT. RATHER,
IT IS A GRADUAL, YET
CONTINUAL "UNFOLDING"
PROCESS.

WEEK 49

Commitments

FAITH

RELATIONSHIPS

WORK

KNOWLEDGE

SOCIETY

FITNESS

LEISURE

*I*T'S ALL ABOUT
BALANCE, WHICH MEANS
MAKING SURE THAT YOU
DEVOTE TIME TO ALL OF
THE 7 LIFEWORK AREAS,
IN THE CONTEXT OF YOUR
PERSONAL VOCATION
AND MISSION.

WEEK *50*

Commitments

FAITH

RELATIONSHIPS

WORK

KNOWLEDGE

SOCIETY

FITNESS

LEISURE

Our faith is a gift from God. At the same time, faith is like a seed. When properly nurtured, the seed grows into something big and beautiful.

LifeWork Role

Role Model

Personal Quality

WEEK *51*

Commitments

FAITH

RELATIONSHIPS

WORK

KNOWLEDGE

SOCIETY

FITNESS

LEISURE

*T*O EXPERIENCE DIVINE
GRACE IS TO KNOW
THE PEACE AND JOY
THAT CAN ONLY COME
FROM GOD. IT IS THE
<u>FAVOR</u>, THE FREE AND
UNDESERVED <u>HELP</u>
THAT GOD GIVES US
TO RESPOND TO HIS
PERSONAL CALL.

WEEK *52*

Commitments

FAITH

RELATIONSHIPS

WORK

KNOWLEDGE

SOCIETY

FITNESS

LEISURE

*T*IME IS TRULY
A GIFT FROM GOD –
THE GIFT OF LIFE
ITSELF!